THE ENTREPRENEUR'S TAX PLAYBOOK (IN PLAIN ENGLISH)

THE ENTREPRENEUR'S TAX PLAYBOOK (IN PLAIN ENGLISH)

No Geek Speak or Tax Codes
Just Proven Strategies to
Maximize Your Wealth

RONALD PARISI, CPA, JD

Published by
Lunch Break Books®
1460 Broadway
New York NY 10036

www.LunchBreakBooks.com

For more information on Lunch Break Books® including to find out how you can become a published author, visit www.LunchBreakBooks.com

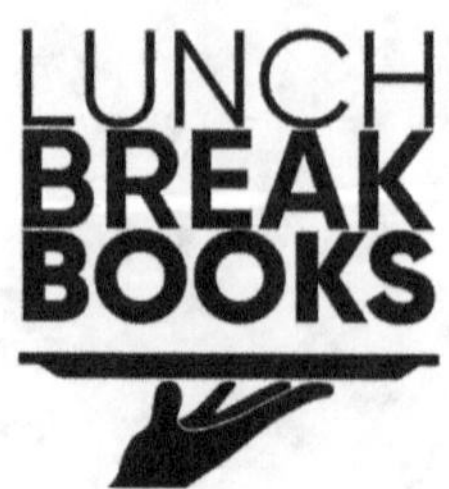

FOREWORD

I've been in the tax game for over 20 years. Yep, two decades of diving deep into the tax maze, decoding the ever-changing tax rules, and helping clients make sense of it all. So, when I came across Ron Parisi's book, it felt like someone had just opened a window in a stuffy room. And let me tell ya, the breath of fresh air was much needed!

Now, don't get me wrong, Ron's not trying to reinvent the wheel here. In fact, what he brings to the table is grounded in common sense. But here's the twist – it's the kind of sense that's been overlooked by so many in our field for so long. Instead of going with the flow and sticking to the traditional, often confusing, ways of thinking about taxes, Ron's gone and thrown in a fresh perspective. It's like he took a step back, looked at the bigger picture, and said, "Hey, why are we making this so complicated?"

One thing I genuinely loved about the book? The realness. Ron's not just throwing tax jargon at you. He shares stories, like the one about Cindy, that show what happens when you don't plan ahead. We've all been there, right? A surprise tax bill, a last-minute scramble – it's the stuff of nightmares for entrepreneurs. But through Ron's guidance, you'll see there's a better way to do things.

Plus, his casual, straight-to-the-point approach makes you feel like you're having a coffee chat with a buddy who happens to know a ton about taxes. He's on a mission to help entrepreneurs, especially those in the tricky phase of growing their businesses. Whether you're an entrepreneur yourself or someone like me, deep in the tax world, there's a nugget (or ten) in here for you.

This isn't just another tax book. It's a friendly nudge, a reminder that sometimes, common sense and a fresh outlook can make all the difference.

TIM CISTONE
Bottomline CPA
Dublin, OH

"*The hardest thing in the world to understand is the income tax.*"

ALBERT EINSTEIN

CONTENTS

INTRODUCTION

I have to begin this book with some words of admiration: I applaud your commitment to your business's financial health and to building your personal wealth. Your dedication is impressive! I mean, it's so strong that you've picked up a book on *taxes*. And very few people—even among growth-obsessed entrepreneurs like you—enjoy reading (or even thinking) about taxes.

So, kudos to you.

Next, I want to make some promises: In this book, I'll keep things concise and to-the-point. We won't be getting lost in a jungle of esoteric tax codes, and we won't be charting a dangerous path through risky tax schemes. Rather, I'll be serving as your expert guide through the business tax landscape. Along the way, I'll point out dangers and misconceptions to avoid, and I'll show you some tried-and-true routes to financial success and maximum wealth.

One thing there won't be? Shortcuts. As we'll discuss, tax planning requires dynamic long-term thinking.

This book is about navigating your taxes with the right (and, of course, always legal) strategies and—equally as important—the right mindset.

Knowing Me, Knowing You

For those of you who've picked up this book after reading *Financial Superpowers*, the first book in this series, welcome back. For those of you who are meeting me for the first time, allow me to introduce myself. I'm an entrepreneur who's also had a fast-track corporate career in finance, and I'm the CEO of CPA On Fire, a financial advisory company that specializes in working with high-performing entrepreneurs and growing businesses. I created a system called "The Entrepreneur's Business Wealth Maximizer Methodology" to help entrepreneurs and business owners like you grow their wealth.

That's because I understand where you are (or where you soon hope to be) and what you need: You're a CEO/founder with a small privately held business (or maybe two or three businesses) with annual revenue in the area of $1 million to $10 million. You're looking for VC funding, or thinking about an exit, or perhaps looking for new ways to build your wealth. With only a handful of employees, you probably don't have a CFO. Maybe you have a controller, maybe you work with a CPA firm, or maybe you have a bookkeeper. But as far as tax strategy, you're figuring a lot out on your own—a huge pain point, and the source of a lot of stress, because the more your wealth grows, the more tax "surprises" you encounter.

And it's very likely that you're going about your taxes all wrong— and putting your personal wealth at risk.

Thinking Differently about Taxes

Taxes are going to be your number one expense over the course of your lifetime. If you look back at your past tax-time behavior with this idea in mind, you may already be seeing some errors in the way you think about them.

I work frequently with entrepreneurs, and they typically fall into one of three mindset categories:

1. They're totally winging it—their tax bills are always larger than they expect, they don't know whether they're fully compliant with tax laws and regulations, and the thought of an audit is intensely terrifying. (This haphazard approach will likely lead to substantial tax liabilities.)

2. They're making a minimal effort—they're doing some planning, but only in the short term, and their focus is on taking the maximum possible deductions on this year's taxes. They're the kind of people you often see buying a big-ticket item like a Tesla on December 15, to get the bonus depreciation—not a good tactic, as we'll discuss later. (This focus on immediate returns will likely lead to a higher tax burden in the long run.)

3. They're on the right track—they have long-term tax strategies in place, they have a clear view into the future, and they're making realistic but flexible plans to build their business or businesses and grow their wealth. (This is where I want to get you.)

Let's consider an example—we'll call her Cindy. She's been working very hard on her business for three years. She held steady for the first two years, but in the third year, her company's profitability and revenues really took off. But that year, Cindy did what she'd always done with profits: She reinvested them into her business, without considering the tax implications. In late February, as usual, she gave her tax preparer all the previous year's paperwork.

In April, her tax professional let her know that she had a significant tax liability for the previous year.

Caught completely off guard, Cindy was forced to make difficult sacrifices in order to pay her tax bill, and those sacrifices affected her company's ability to grow (and had a deleterious effect on her personal wealth as well).

I see this kind of thing all the time. A lack of long-term planning has led Cindy seriously astray.

Having a multiple-year tax strategy is crucial because the business environment (and tax law) is always changing. And as I discussed in my book *Financial Superpowers*, having a clear view of your business's current performance (by tracking the right metrics) is also key. If you can't clearly see where you are in relation to where want to go, you won't know how to correct course when something unexpected shows up in your path.

Charting the Road Ahead

I wrote this book with business owners and entrepreneurs like you in mind, because your needs when it comes to taxes are unique. I hope that when you finish reading it, you will be better equipped to map out your tax journey. We'll discuss the importance of understanding progressive taxation, the pitfalls of appreciation and depreciation, how to "think like a rich person," how to identify a competent tax preparer (they are definitely not all created equal), and the right (and wrong) ways to think about tax-preparation software.

I look forward to taking these next steps with you on your path to becoming an empowered, financially savvy entrepreneur.

"I have lived by one crucial principle since I was 24 years old. I don't blame or complain about things like the economy, the government, taxes, employees, gas prices, or any of the external things that I don't have control over. The only thing I have control over is my response to these things."

JACK CANFIELD

TAX POP QUIZ

Hey Entrepreneur,

This book **will NOT help you with your taxes *whatsoever*,** unless, of course one of these scenarios applies to you:

1. You're feeling lost in the maze of your company's finances and tax rules. You wish you had a GPS to quickly maneuver you through the dry boring tax codes and distill everything down into what works for your personal and professional situation.

2. You have that sinking feeling that you're missing out on some stealth tax savings strategies that are already known to most of the world's most successful entrepreneurs, but for whatever reason have been kept hidden from you.

3. You hate surprise tax bills. You would rather be getting a root canal at your dentist's office than a letter from the IRS telling you that not only do you owe them more money, but that your interest is accruing interest.

4. You've been in survival mode during tax time, pushing for the biggest deductions without feeling tax optimized. You're not sure how to change that.

5. You're a true entrepreneur, with the scars to prove it. You know your business can go much, *much* further, but you need a handle on financial and tax strategy.

6. You're tired of Googling tax questions without finding real expert advice...yet.

Still reading? Great – let's dive in!

"Like mothers, taxes are often misunderstood, but seldom forgotten."

LORD BRAMWELL

UNDERSTANDING THE PHASES OF YOUR BUSINESS'S LIFE

*"What lies behind us, and what lies before us,
are tiny matters compared to what lies within us."*

—RALPH WALDO EMERSON

When you own a small or growing business, taxes can start to get unpleasantly complex, right? But if you look at this situation another way, one of the *joys* of being a business owner is that you have a lot more flexibility—and many more opportunities, such as business credits and business deductions—when it comes to managing your tax liability.

A business typically has five phases of life—and note that when I say this, I mean *all* businesses, whether we're talking about a hot Silicon Valley tech startup or a small family business in rural Indiana. Each phase of life has different needs and opportunities when it comes to tax planning.

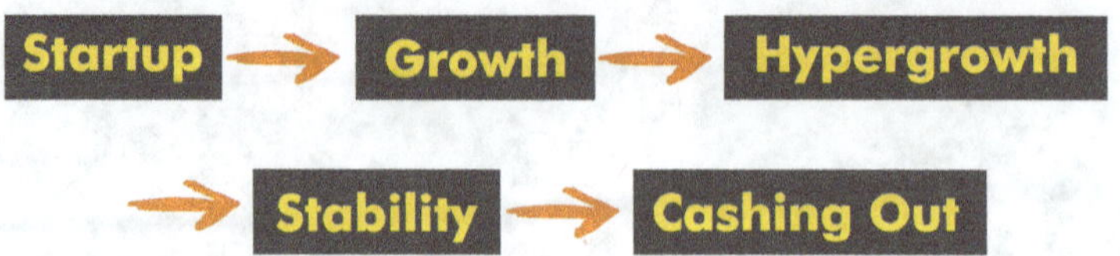

It's important to match your tax strategy with the phase of life that your business is in, as well as to consider the optimal structure for your business as it grows—from an LLC (Schedule C) to an S-Corp (better for smaller, domestic businesses), and then to a C-Corp (better for larger companies, because C-Corps allow for more flexibility when it comes to ownership and profit distribution) or a partnership. Each structure has different advantages and benefits that are well suited to different stages.

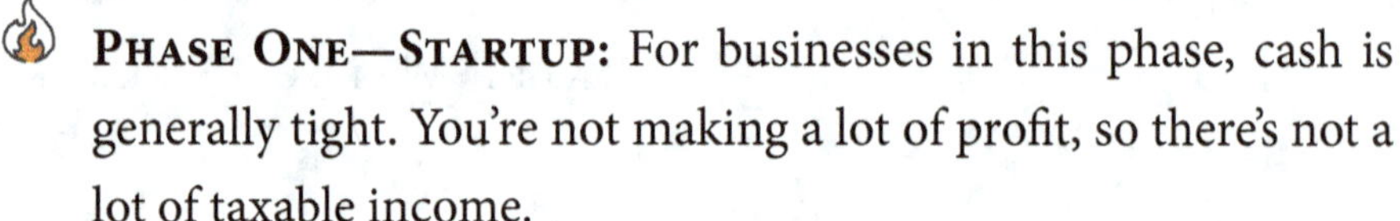

PHASE ONE—STARTUP: For businesses in this phase, cash is generally tight. You're not making a lot of profit, so there's not a lot of taxable income.

PHASE TWO—GROWTH: When your business is in this phase, you're just carefully putting one foot in front of the other. A bit of cash is coming in, but you're investing any money that you make back into the business. As in the first phase, there's not a lot of profitability and therefore not a lot of taxable income.

PHASE THREE—HYPERGROWTH: The third phase begins when your business really finds its groove—when you've found your place in the market. Customers understand you, they like you, and they're buying from you. So, suddenly you have surplus cash—during this phase, revenue is increasing at an exponential rate. This is when you start looking for opportunities: Maybe you're expanding your real estate portfolio and are buying a commercial building or an event space. In this phase and the one that follows—when you have surplus cash—tax planning becomes very important. Many more strategies become available to you because you don't need to use all your cash just to keep your business alive.

 **PHASE FOUR—STABILITY:** For a business in this phase, cash flow becomes predictable. You're continuing to grow, but at a steadier rate for which you can project and plan. Of all the phases, this one is perhaps the most important in terms of tax planning. Because your cash flow is relatively predictable, you can start making longer-term strategic plans.

 **PHASE FIVE—CASHING OUT:** When you reach this stage of your business, a next step is typically looking at a couple of different paths: If you want to stay involved in the business, you think about VC financing; if you don't, you start thinking about selling your company.

I'll reiterate—all businesses go through these phases, and knowing which one your business is in will help you maximize profits and your own personal wealth.

Imagine someone who's just taken over a small but profitable family plumbing business that has been operating smoothly for thirty years. They think of it as "the family business," and they run it as it has always been run and have their taxes done by the same family friend who's always done them. But if they look at this plumbing business as a company in the fourth phase of its life, new tax strategy opportunities may become apparent.

The purpose of the book is to raise awareness about the possibilities available to business owners like you. This is not a DIY tax-preparation manual—and by the way, be very wary of those! Instead, I want this book to help you think about your business in a different way, so you can approach your finances strategically and with the right mindset.

Think Like a Wealthy Person

Short-term thinking is one of the biggest mistakes I see entrepreneurs and business owners make—they act as if the primary goal of tax planning is to maximize their deductions every year. What they *should* be doing is maximizing legal tax advantages that align with their business goals (and personal wealth goals).

In other words, they should be thinking like a rich person.

Before CPA On Fire, I worked at a Big Four accounting firm and assisted some of the wealthiest people in the world with their finances—I'm talking about people with substantial wealth going back generations. Seeing what they do and how they think informs how I work with entrepreneurs and help them bring their own wealth to another level.

Wealthy people think about the long game. The typical business owner looks only into the near future (or worse, only in the rearview mirror).

The mistake those business owners make is thinking, "I just want to minimize this year's tax bill in any way possible." But if they look just a few years out, maybe they'll see that a little pain this year could lead to larger rewards down the line. Just as an example, we're potentially talking about the difference between taking advantage of every possible bonus and depreciation this year and getting a 10 percent tax break on a new piece of equipment—and spreading out the depreciation over three years and getting a 37 percent tax break on it instead.

To make decisions like this, you need to understand the options available to you—and many traditional tax preparers are not going to help you do that. They're looking at a $100,000 business expense, and instead of saving you $37,000 dollars over three years, they're automatically going to save you $10,000 right now.

Let's consider a business owner we'll call Mike. Mike owns a specialty manufacturing company that makes parts for electric vehicles. He's in something of a niche market, but he's having a very good year. Unexpectedly, a big order comes in for which he needs a new CAD machine. The machine costs $300,000, but he doesn't have the cash on hand, so he puts 50 percent down and takes out a loan from an unconventional lender with super high interest rates for the rest. Now, with an investment that large, most business owners (and tax preparers) are going to be looking for an immediate deduction. But Mike is doing well, and this big order is proof of that. So, he needs to ask himself, "Is there a longer-term tax strategy that will have a better impact on my business and on my personal wealth?"

Think of all you've built with your company—think of the blood, sweat, and tears you've invested, the countless and priceless hours. By that measure, your company is already worth a fortune. So, it's time to think like a wealthy person and maximize your company's value by paying close attention to its biggest expense.

In the next chapter, we'll talk more about thinking like a rich person—and playing the long game when it comes to your taxes.

"*Philosophy teaches a man
that he can't take it with him;
taxes teach him he can't leave
it behind either.*"

C H A P T E R   T W O

PLAYING THE LONG GAME

"Plans are nothing; planning is everything."

—Dwight D. Eisenhower

Rich people strategize their wealth building over years—generations, even. Therefore, it only makes sense: If you want to be rich, you need to do the same thing.

And planning your taxes over multiple years is part of that longer-term thinking. The overarching goal is to reduce your tax liability by planning over a span of time, rather than just taking the most advantageous deductions when you file your taxes every April.

For instance, as you're working with your tax preparer, you should be able to ask them, as you look at each deduction, "Might there be a greater tax savings or a lower liability if we make this deduction next year or the year after?"

From growth to hypergrowth to stability, you need to look for the various strategies that will be available to you at each of your business's phases.

Now, there are lots of differences in tax codes from state to state (and things change from year to year as well), so I'm talking about a mindset more than I'm talking about particulars. Just keep in mind that the behaviors that got your business to $1 or $2 million in revenue are probably not going to take it to the next level.

Marginal Tax Rates vs. Effective Tax Rates

Many small business owners understand their marginal tax rates. This is the tax rate that's applied to each dollar earned: For instance, if your business's tax rate is 25 percent and you earn $10,000, your marginal tax obligation is $2,500.

But when you're doing long-term planning for taxes, you should also be considering your effective tax rate—the amount you expect to actually pay.

For instance, if a small business has a total income of $100,000 and ends up paying $20,000 in taxes, their effective tax rate is 20 percent (even though their marginal tax rate might be 25 percent). The effective tax rate is a more comprehensive view of a business's tax liability, as it takes into account the effects of various tax strategies and deductions on the amount paid in taxes.

Depreciation

We'll talk more about allowed and allowable depreciation in a later chapter, but I also wanted to bring it up here, because ignorance of this concept can really bite you in the … well, let's say it can bite you in the wallet.

Depreciation is a type of annual tax deduction that allows you to recover financial losses due to deterioration or obsolescence of property or other assets—such as machinery.

Remember Mike, the specialty manufacturer from the last chapter? He bought a CAD machine for $300,000, but after three years of wear and tear, it will be worth a lot less than that, and he can claim the difference in value on his taxes.

As a business owner, you're allowed to claim depreciation on certain assets when you file your taxes—and if you *don't* claim depreciation in a year in which you are allowed to do so, you can't claim it the following year. It's complex, and as I say, we'll come back to depreciation later. For now, just know that whether you take the deduction or not, the IRS is going to view it as having been taken. There's no turning back the clock.

Progressive Tax Rates

Another thing you need to understand when you think about playing the long game is progressive tax rates—basically, as you make more money, your tax rates increase. So as your business becomes more successful (in other words, as it enters the third phase of life, hypergrowth), you run the risk of being surprised by a hefty tax bill if you're not planning ahead.

For instance, say you habitually put aside 20 percent of your profits to cover taxes—after a year of hypergrowth, your tax liability could be closer to 35% or 40%, or even higher. It's important to always be conscious of how your business is performing and what those thresholds for higher tax rates currently are.

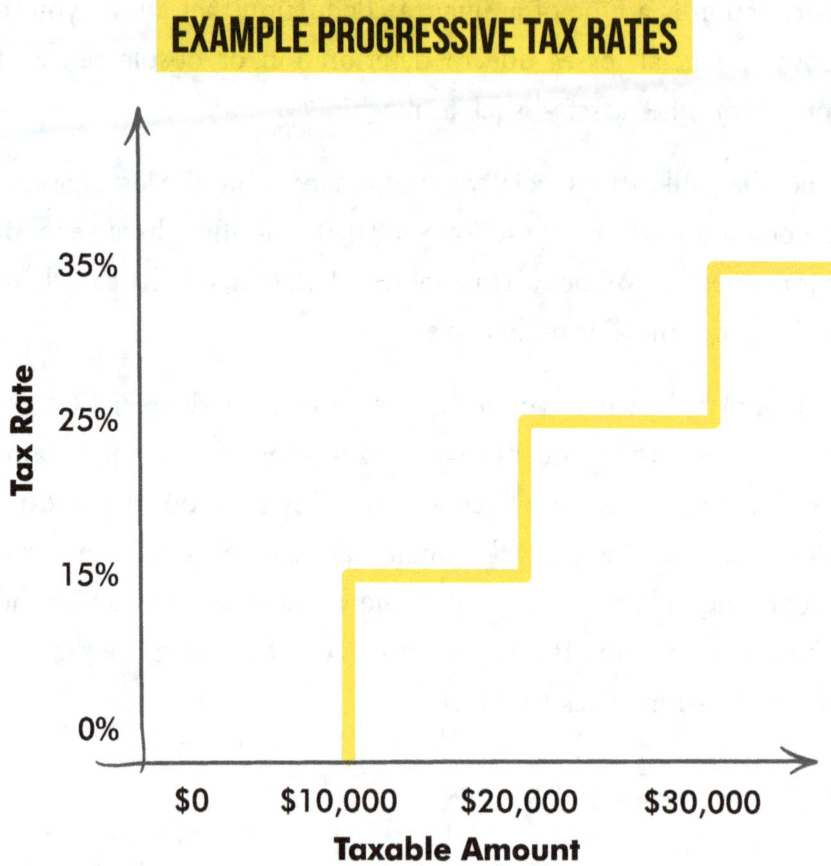

Plus, other taxes may start kicking in as your business becomes more successful—so without planning ahead, you could end up paying more than 50 percent of your business income in taxes. Today, in year two, your business may be at a 24 percent rate—but keep in mind that in year four, it might be in the 50 percent bracket. So, what are you doing today to make sure that you're not reporting all taxable income in year four, when you're in that higher tax bracket?

This is why you make a plan: You have to balance today's cash needs (fulfilling orders, paying employees, and so on) with your future expectations.

Do the Work Now, Pay Less Later

Saving on your taxes takes discipline. For instance, say you want to take advantage of the Augusta rule. Otherwise known as Section 280A, this IRS rule allows you to rent your home back to your business for up to fourteen days in a calendar year without being taxed on the rental income. Good deal, right? But to take advantage of this legal loophole, you need to save receipts, draw up a lease agreement, and so on.

And successful financial planning requires keeping cash on hand for expenses that might come up, whether that's having to replace a pricey piece of equipment, buying one of your competitors when it suddenly becomes available for purchase, or just paying a high tax bill after an unexpectedly good year.

As an example, let's consider an entrepreneur we'll call Pam. She recently left an executive position at a national nonprofit and founded a consultancy for nonprofits. During her first year, she was in the startup phase, and things were a bit of a struggle. In her second year, she hit her growth phase and saw some profits. That increased revenue put her tax rate at 25 percent, and her tax preparer advised her to prepay her office rent and other costs for an immediate deduction. But now, in her third year, she has landed two big new clients—which pushed her into a higher tax bracket: 35 percent. Unfortunately, this year, she doesn't have expenses to offset that higher tax bill, due to the bad advice she got from her tax preparer last year.

Or consider Dennis. In year two of his business's life, he started a solo 401k, and he was maximizing his employee and employer payroll deductions to keep his taxes down. But then one of Dennis's competitors came up for sale, and he had no way to purchase it because his money was tied up in his 401k. And then he moved into a higher tax bracket and was unable to make some necessary purchases that would have made for useful deductions.

So, Dennis saved a bit in taxes, only to lose out on increased profits later on.

To sum this chapter up, when you're doing your tax planning, always be thinking about what's over the horizon—not only what's likely, but also what might happen if you're lucky (or, and I hope this is not the case for you, unlucky). In the next chapter, we're going to talk about a key investment for businesses in the hypergrowth phase of life.

"Why does a slight tax increase cost you two hundred dollars and a substantial tax cut save you thirty cents?"

CHAPTER THREE

INVESTING IN REAL ESTATE DURING YOUR BUSINESS'S HYPERGROWTH PHASE

"Buy land; they're not making it anymore."

—MARK TWAIN

A lot happens during a business's hypergrowth stage—obviously, one big change is increased revenue. Suddenly, your business is profitable! And to put my own spin on the lyrics of a popular song: more money, more *opportunities*.

And one of those opportunities is investing in real estate, which is an excellent way to grow your personal wealth and reduce your tax liability. That real estate could come in the form of office space, event space, or mixed-use space. It could be space that you use entirely for your business, or it could be space that you rent out fully or partially.

No matter how you use the space, there are many different mechanisms for creating deductions based on real estate investments.

One example, a 1031 exchange: If a business owner sells property that they own and then reinvests the proceeds into a replacement property, the transaction has no immediate tax consequence. They can defer any capital gains taxes associated with the sale.

The Right Time to Invest

If you can identify a business need for commercial real estate and have the cash available to make an investment, the time to invest could very well be right now.

Let's say that you hold events—for instance, yearly conventions, or monthly seminars or workshops for your clients—and renting space at hotels and convention centers is getting expensive as attendance at and interest in your events grow. Buying a commercial space, a property that could not only meet your needs but also potentially be rented out to others, might make sense.

One of CPA On Fire's clients has exactly done that: They've purchased a commercial building that they use for their business, but on the weekends, they rent it out as an event space for weddings.

Or think about your corporate offices: Is your rent so high that it might make more sense to just buy the building and pay yourself the rent (while building equity in the real estate)? If you expect your business to grow, you could buy something a bit larger than you need, and until you grow into it, rent part of it out to another small business or to multiple people as a short-term coworking space.

These are the kinds of calculations that you need to do when your business is in its hypergrowth phase. (So start thinking about them *before* you get there—remember, always be planning ahead!) By taking advantage of various real estate tax deductions, you can lessen the carrying costs of real estate in a big way.

Pitfalls to Watch Out For, Mistakes to Avoid

Keep in mind that real estate losses cannot typically offset business income—there are very specific rules about this, and the hoops through which you must jump make it impractical for most businesses.

Be careful not to overleverage yourself and your business, or to put yourself in a "robbing Peter to pay Paul" scenario. You need to be on solid financial footing before investing in real estate so you're able to mitigate the risks of taking on additional liability and cash flow requirements should unexpected problems arise. This requires a detailed analysis of your financial landscape, and those calculations should always start with what you're currently paying for your office rental, your conference space, and so on.

If you're getting into commercial real estate for the first time, be aware that there are important differences between commercial real estate and residential real estate (which you may already be familiar with). For instance, while appreciation and cash flow from commercial real estate tend to be better (because businesses sign long-term leases and can afford higher rent payments than individuals), the costs of operating a commercial property tend to be higher for investors.

It's also important to educate yourself about the "friction costs" of owning and operating commercial real estate: accounting needs, regulatory needs, tax forms, tax filings, and so on.

A Tale of Two Entrepreneurs

Imagine two independent marketing consultants; we'll call one Zack and the other Zoe. They both specialize in working with small businesses to help them grow, and they both love hosting seminars and workshops for clients, potential clients, and other people in their industry. Let's say that these events typically draw between a hundred and two hundred people.

Zack believes that hosting his events in a banquet hall at a fancy hotel gives his events a level of panache, so a large portion of his earnings from these events goes back to the hotel every time.

But Zoe sees the potential in owning her own space—something she can customize for her events. She holds only a couple of events each month, so when she's not using the space, she makes it available for short-term rentals via an online platform, something like Airbnb, that lets people rent working spaces of many different types (for people who need somewhere to have a meeting, party, audition, photo shoot, or what have you).

Having this space allows Zoe to take all sorts of tax deductions, and as her needs grow, she can do a progressive series of 1031 exchanges as she buys larger properties. And when she's ready to step back from her consulting business, her real estate investment will become an excellent source of passive income for her.

My goal for this chapter is simply to open your eyes to the opportunities real estate may provide as your business grows—it's an avenue that too many entrepreneurs overlook! Up next, we'll get into more ways to save on taxes and manage your cash.

"Dear IRS, I am writing to you to cancel my subscription. Please remove my name from your mailing list."

CHAPTER FOUR

MANAGING YOUR CASH AND MAXIMIZING YOUR TAX SAVINGS

"A man who both spends and saves money is the happiest man, because he has both enjoyments."

—SAMUEL JOHNSON

As a business owner, you have unique opportunities to grow your personal wealth and save on your taxes. But if you want to grow your business, you also need to be sure that you are managing your cash well and keeping reserves of cash available, so you can take advantage of opportunities when they present themselves.

We've just discussed real estate, and that's definitely an opportunity that you want to be prepared to jump on. It's one of the "big three" for entrepreneurs; the other two are business acquisitions (for instance, if one of your competitors goes up for sale) and human resources (being able to hire well as your staffing needs grow is crucial for a growing business).

Keeping Your Cash in the Family

One great example of a smart way to take cash out of your business and turn it into personal wealth is to hire your kids.

As an example, let's consider Zoe, the fictional marketing consultant from the previous chapter. She has twin teenage sons, Jesse and Jimmy. She hires her sons and pays each of them $6,000 to help her at her events throughout the year—setting up the space, checking people in at the registration table, keeping the coffee urns and water pitchers full, and so on.

That $6,000 amount for each child is lower than their standard deduction, and she can put all or some of that money right into a 529 account (a college savings account), where it will grow on a tax-deferred basis. This way, Zoe is not only saving on taxes but also investing in her family's future.

Of course, not everyone has kids. But using your own Roth IRA to keep and grow your wealth is a similar strategy: You're investing money you earn from your business into a personal retirement account, a very smart way to use your business to grow your personal wealth and defer taxes.

Again, it's crucial to make sure that you don't tie all your cash up in investment vehicles where it can't be accessed. Managing your finances means balancing your business needs with your personal goals—and you can't do that properly without taking a long view of your finances.

It's an idea we keep returning to: It's all about thinking like a rich person.

Different Strategies for Different Business Life Phases

Understanding what stage of life your business is in will help you make decisions about which strategies are right for you.

Typically, strategies like putting money into longer-term tax-deferment accounts like 529s and Roth IRAs will make sense when your business is in the growth or hypergrowth phase.

Then other strategies will come later: For instance, a cash balance pension plan might make sense for a business in the fourth or fifth phase of life (stability or cashing out).

So how do you know when and how to make decisions like this? As we'll discuss in the next chapter, it's all about making sure that you have the right people on your team.

"The flat tax would be so simple, you could fill it out on a post card. A post card that would say, in effect, having a wonderful time; glad most of my money is here."

STEVE FORBES

CHAPTER FIVE

CHOOSING THE RIGHT TAX PREPARER

*"Great things in business are never done by one
person; they're done by a team of people."*

—STEVE JOBS

In the introduction to this book, I mentioned that not all tax preparers are created equal. And now I'll let you in on a little-known fact of the financial world: It's very easy (I'd say that it's far *too* easy) to hang out a tax-preparation shingle, take on clients, and start filing taxes for them.

Many states don't have any licensing requirements at all for paid tax preparers—as of this writing, only seven states regulate them. On a national level, the IRS requires very little of someone before authorizing them to prepare and file taxes on behalf of clients: Basically, you pay a small registration fee to get an IRS Preparer Tax Identification Number (PTIN) … and that's about it.

So how do you choose a great tax professional? First, you may have to make sure that they have the appropriate credentials. Although anyone can *prepare* your taxes, only three classes of tax preparers have the right to represent you before the IRS if there is a dispute of some kind:

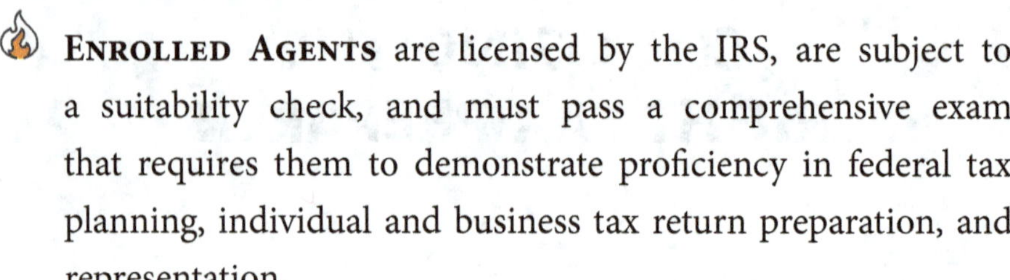

- **ENROLLED AGENTS** are licensed by the IRS, are subject to a suitability check, and must pass a comprehensive exam that requires them to demonstrate proficiency in federal tax planning, individual and business tax return preparation, and representation.

- **CERTIFIED PUBLIC ACCOUNTANTS** are licensed by state boards. They must have completed college- or university-level studies in accounting, and they must participate in continuing education (and meet other standards set by their local boards) to maintain licensing.

- **ATTORNEYS** are licensed by state boards or their designees. Generally, they have earned a degree in law and passed a bar exam and must meet other requirements. Some attorneys specialize in tax preparation and planning.

Second, you have to make sure that the tax preparer you choose understands your needs as the owner of a small business. Like you, they should be taking a long view: working with a multiple-year, flexible plan (and thinking like a rich person).

Ask yourself these questions:

- "How often is my tax preparer meeting with me?" (By the way, the right answer here is "At least quarterly, not just in February.")

 "Does my tax preparer respond in a timely way to me, by email or phone, when I have questions? (They should respond within a couple of business days.)

 "Do they offer me alternatives, with clear explanations of pros and cons, when it comes to tax deductions, credits, and so on?" (They should be doing their best to make sure you understand all your options.)

 "Is my tax preparer familiar with the entrepreneurial mindset?" (You can ask them about their other small-business clients to find out.)

You don't want to find yourself in a situation where your tax preparer is just looking at spreadsheets and punching numbers into their accounting program! If you're not working with someone who understands entrepreneurs, understands the life phases of a growing business, and knows what opportunities and pitfalls are out there, you could end up losing hundreds of thousands of dollars.

As with entrepreneurs, there are three types of tax preparers:

1. They're doing the bare minimum—their work is reactive. It's tax preparation only, no real tax planning. Their focus is typically on compliance (checking the right boxes and sending the right forms, but not really looking out for their clients).

2. They're making a minimal effort—they're doing some planning, but only in the short term. They're maximizing current strategies, such as retirement planning and an annual review of deductions, without any real concept of a multiple-year plan.

3. They're thinking in the long term—there's foresight, there's planning, and there are real-time responses to changes in your business and in the business environment. They have an understanding of the entrepreneurial mindset, and they are truly part of your team. (This is the type of tax preparer I want you to work with!)

A Cautionary Tale

As an example, let's look at the founder of a digital marketing agency—we'll call her Hazel. Hazel has an uncle who does taxes, her Uncle Stan. So, every year in February, she just hands her documents over to Stan, he files her taxes, and she writes a check to the IRS as needed. Hazel and Stan see each other at holiday dinners and other family occasions, and they have a great relationship, but Hazel finds tax talk boring—and to be honest, Stan does, too. Frankly, he's just running out the clock as he looks forward to his imminent retirement.

For the past couple of years, Hazel has been paying between $150,000 and $200,000 in taxes (while her business is making a bit more than half a million dollars). So that annual tax bill is a huge pain point for her.

Finally, Uncle Stan retires—he moves into a new condo in Hilton Head Island, South Carolina, and he gets serious about his golf game. He's happy, and Hazel is happy for him.

Then she takes her taxes to the team at my company, CPA On Fire, and we create a five-year tax savings plan for her at the very start of the year. And now, because Hazel has a much more strategic view of her long-term goals, and they're aligned with her strategies, she's paying a much lower tax rate overall (and thereby increasing her wealth).

In addition, she's shocked to learn exactly how badly Uncle Stan has hurt her business over the past few years. (Sadly, you can only amend tax returns going back three years.)

For instance, Uncle Stan didn't have entrepreneurial expertise, so he didn't even know that Hazel could have taken a tax credit of 20 percent of her yearly investment in research and development. And in one year, Hazel spent $500,000 on R&D. She didn't take the credit, and that means she lost out on $100,000. (The failure to properly take this R&D credit is a *huge* miss for many entrepreneurs.)

And that's just one of the big misses; there are countless deductions available to business owners as well, and the amounts and options change depending on many factors (such as whether they work at home or rent a separate office space, for instance).

The moral of this cautionary tale? Don't settle for mediocrity when it comes to your business and personal wealth.

And there's a second moral here, as well: Don't let personal relationships get in the way of your success. In the final analysis, this ends up hurting your team, because if you're not growing the company, you're not creating opportunities for your employees. Don't hurt yourself and your business—and by extension the many people who rely on your business—for the sake of one relationship.

*"Our tax code is so
long it makes War and
Peace seem breezy."*

Steven LaTourette

CHAPTER SIX

CREATING YOUR LONG-TERM STRATEGY

*"The future is not something we enter.
The future is something we create."*

—LEONARD I. SWEET

No matter what business you're in, you can think of your business plan as one of a triad of interwoven, complementary strategies; this triad also includes your long-term financial plan and your tax plan.

Because if we've learned anything over the course of this book, it's that achieving goals requires planning—right?

In an ideal world, a business owner will have a five-year plan. But again, we're really talking about a triad of plans: one for their business, one for their finances, and one for their taxes. And then, every quarter or so, they can return to this plan to adjust it and course correct as needed.

You might base changes to your plans on business performance, changes in the market, changes to your team, and so on. The ebbs and flows of business performance will obviously affect your tax planning.

So many factors come into play! As discussed earlier in this book, as your business grows, tax rates get progressively higher—and new strategies become available to you. At different points, real estate and R&D credits may come into play (*don't miss out on R&D credits!*). And ultimately, different retirement options will come into play as well.

And there's more: Are you hiring employees? Are you working from an office? What are the personal wealth management strategies you want to pursue? These are the sorts of questions you'll have to discuss with your tax preparer as you answer them for yourself.

Taking an Active Role in Your Business's Success

Throughout this book, I've focused on the benefits of creating a long-term tax plan. So now you may be asking, "But what does that commitment look like for me?" And the answer is … "Well, it depends!"

It depends on a few factors—including how clear your vision of the future is. Let's say that clarifying this vision is the first step. As a tax professional, I'd expect to take a few hours over two or three meetings with an entrepreneur to clarify their vision and to then set up their financial plan and tax plan.

A few hours is typically how long it takes for me to get a solid understanding of what the client's ultimate financial goals are, where the business is, and what the business's trajectory is.

Then I'd expect to have a check-in meeting every quarter or so (I'd plan for about an hour), so both my client and I can stay on top of current conditions and their progress toward their goals.

And no matter how your business is currently structured, whether it's an S-Corp, a C-Corp, or a partnership, it's important for me to look at the interplay between the business and the business owner—because the business affects the person, and vice versa.

A Couple of Example Scenarios

As a first example, let's talk about a company that's doing everything right when it comes to long-term tax planning. We'll say it's a small local chain of dental clinics in Philadelphia, and it's currently transitioning from its hypergrowth phase into its stability phase.

If I were advising this business owner on their tax strategy, the first thing I'd do is plot out the next five years of the business in terms of desired and projected growth and figure out what's needed to fuel that growth. It's crucial to really understand not only the P&L statement but also the balance sheet.

For instance, what kind of equipment will they need to invest in? Say they're looking to grow their chain of clinics from three Philadelphia locations to four, and then to open three new locations in Pennsylvania: one in Wilkes-Barre; one in Harrisburg; and one in Scranton. What are those buildouts going to look like? Are they buying existing practices or starting from scratch? (And for companies in that hypergrowth phase, you always have to look at cash, because growth typically burns through cash.)

The answers to these questions will help me form a budget and a forecast, so we can make calculations and projections, not only at the business level, but also at the personal level. We need to figure out how the business will affect the entrepreneur in terms of their tax liabilities and so on, and then we see what strategies are available, always taking into account the need for cash on hand.

As a second example, think of an emerging business—say it's a small tech company that's still in startup mode, still scratching their way to that $1 million mark. As a tax preparer, I would still start out looking at business projections and thinking about that five-year plan, but the needs of a company at this stage are different.

For example, where tax planning becomes very important for a startup is in terms of the employee count and what type of team they're going to put together. This will have an effect on the strategies that are available to them. A company in startup mode usually has one or two employees and uses a lot of consultants or freelancers, but eventually, they're going to need to build their own team. And employing people creates some opportunities and limits others.

In both scenarios, my goal is, at the core, to understand what's projected to happen with the business so that I can map out the strategies that are going to be available to them as the business grows.

Mistakes to Watch Out For

I see entrepreneurs make mistakes in three primary areas. The first, perhaps the biggest, is having the mindset that simply making enough money will solve all their problems (without planning, it won't!).

The second is poor timing—taking advantage of tax credits or deductions too early or too late.

And the third is just not doing proper forecasting—not having a clear view of what's on the horizon for the business. You can't drive your car properly if you're focused on the rearview mirror.

A Happy Ending

As another example, let's consider Skyler. Skyler is a serial entrepreneur who struggles with bridging the gap between his accounting people and his tax people. It consumes energy, it consumes time, and he's not very good at playing an intermediary role in the first place—he'd rather be out there making the deals. And then Skyler eventually finds this amazing accounting firm, CPA On Fire. They give him accurate financials he can understand. They use those projections to create a long-term strategy. Now he's saving an incredible amount of time. He's elevating the company's operations. And his tax liabilities are the lowest they've been in years.

This is my goal for you, whether you work with CPA On Fire or not—that you're able to use the key ideas in this book to successfully grow your business and manage your tax strategy. So, I'll close this chapter with a refresher of the key ideas in this book:

 Your business has different needs throughout its life cycle. It's important to match your tax strategy with the phase of life that your business is in, as well as to consider the optimal structure for your business as it grows.

 Think like a rich person, and always be playing the long game when it comes to your taxes. You should have a plan and strategies that reach multiple years into the future.

 When you are thinking about investing, always consider real estate!

 As a business owner, you have unique opportunities to grow your personal wealth and save on your taxes. But be sure to balance long-term investments with keeping reserves of cash available, so you can take advantage of opportunities when they present themselves.

 Not all tax preparers are created equal! Choose yours carefully, and make sure that they know how to meet the special needs of growth-minded entrepreneurs. Watch out for tax preparers who are only reactive, not proactive.

 Create a long-term strategy for your taxes. No matter what business you're in, you can think of your business plan as one of a triad of interwoven, complementary strategies; this triad also includes your long-term financial plan and your tax plan.

Still have questions? Not to worry! In the next section, I'm going to walk you through some mistakes to avoid, and then I'll guide you through a tax quiz that will help you better understand your own tax needs.

DON'T MAKE THESE COMMON ENTREPRENEUR TAX MISTAKES

Mistake One: "Our company already has a tax accountant, aren't I doing everything I can to manage my tax liabilities?

While having a tax accountant suggests that you're hopefully tax compliant, it rarely means that you're "tax strategic". Here are a few things to consider:

1. **SCOPE OF SERVICE:** Not all tax accountants provide the same level of service. Some may focus primarily on compliance (ensuring you meet all legal obligations) and are not true tax specialists with a very advanced level of knowledge about how to best plan your taxes to minimize liabilities.

2. **EXPERTISE:** The world of taxation is a vast and deep ocean, and while a tax accountant might be well-versed in general tax code, they might not be specialized in a specific industry. For instance, there could be industry-specific deductions or incentives that they're not familiar with such as eCommerce businesses, marketing agencies, internet coaching companies and so on.

3. **STRATEGIC PLANNING:** There's a grand-canyon sized difference between short-term tax reductions and long-term tax strategy. Simply taking every deduction available in a given year might not be the best strategy for your overall financial health in the long run.

4. **COMMUNICATION:** Regular communication with your accountant is crucial. They should be aware of your business plans, investments, and any other financial changes. Does he or she strategically contribute to your business plans? Only with full information can they strategize effectively for tax minimization.

In summary, while having a tax accountant is a step in the right direction, it's step 1 of a hundred mile tax journey. It's essential to ensure that they're not just ensuring compliance but also proactively helping you strategize to minimize tax liabilities effectively.

Mistake Two: I don't have time to worry about taxes and finances, I want to maximize my growth.

As the founder, you spend the majority of your time on your product/service and marketing/sales. Understanding and managing taxes and accounting is crucial for entrepreneurs for several reasons:

1. **FINANCIAL HEALTH:** Even if you're generating significant revenue, improper tax and accounting management can lead to financial strain or losses. Properly managed finances provide a clear picture of your business's actual profitability.

2. **LEGAL COMPLIANCE:** Tax regulations are strict, and non-compliance can result in hefty penalties, fines, or legal actions. Being informed ensures that you're adhering to all necessary

laws and regulations, preventing any unwelcome surprises during tax season.

3. **DECISION MAKING:** Accurate accounting gives insight into your business's financial health, helping you make informed decisions. Whether it's about expansion, hiring, investment, or cutting costs, having clear financial data is crucial.

4. **CASH FLOW MANAGEMENT:** Understanding your tax obligations and having a clear accounting system allows you to manage your cash flow better, ensuring that you have enough funds to cover operational costs, including tax liabilities.

5. **LONG-TERM SAVINGS:** Strategic tax planning can lead to significant savings over the long run. By understanding available deductions, credits, and incentives, you can effectively reduce your tax liabilities.

6. **ATTRACTING INVESTORS:** If you're looking for external funding, investors will want to see well-maintained financial records. Proper accounting showcases your business's financial discipline and viability.

7. **EXIT STRATEGY:** If you ever decide to sell your business, having clean and clear financial records can increase its valuation and make the sales process smoother.

8. **PEACE OF MIND:** Knowing that your finances are in order and you're prepared for tax season can reduce stress and allow you to focus on other critical aspects of your business.

While it's understandable that as an entrepreneur, you're juggling multiple tasks, it's essential to either educate yourself on basic tax and accounting principles or hire experts to manage it for you. Consider it an investment in your business's longevity and success – and in your sanity!

Mistake Three: The April Tax Surprise.

Why was I surprised by my HUGE tax bill this year?

There are several reasons why you, as a growing entrepreneur, might be caught off-guard by a large tax bill in April:

1. **INADEQUATE TAX PLANNING:** Some entrepreneurs don't engage in proactive tax planning throughout the year. Without periodic check-ins, it's easy to overlook potential liabilities.

2. **ESTIMATED TAX PAYMENTS:** The IRS requires entrepreneurs and self-employed individuals to make quarterly estimated tax payments if they expect to owe taxes of $1,000 or more. If you underestimated these payments or skipped them altogether, you could face a significant bill in April.

3. **INCREASED PROFITS:** If your business saw a sudden or unexpected increase in profits and you didn't adjust your estimated tax payments accordingly, you could owe more in taxes than anticipated.

4. **MISSED DEDUCTIONS:** Failing to track and claim all allowable business expenses and deductions can result in a higher taxable income, leading to a larger tax bill.

5. **UNDERPAYMENT PENALTIES:** If you didn't pay enough taxes throughout the year, either through withholding or estimated tax payments, the IRS might charge an underpayment penalty.

6. **LATE FILING:** If you filed your taxes after the deadline and didn't request an extension, you might face late-filing penalties in addition to the taxes you owe.

7. **LACK OF PROFESSIONAL GUIDANCE:** Not consulting with a tax professional or CPA might result in missed opportunities for tax savings or misinterpretations of tax regulations.

If you were surprised by a large tax bill, it would be beneficial to review your finances with a tax professional to understand the specifics and plan better for the future.

Mistake Four: I'm so overwhelmed with my taxes - I'm just going to sit on this issue a while longer.

Finding the right person to handle your finances and taxes is crucial for your business's success.

Determine Your Needs: Before you start your search, be clear about what you need. Are you looking for someone to just file your taxes, or do you need comprehensive financial advice and planning?

1. **LOOK FOR PROFESSIONALS WITH DESIGNATIONS:** Certified Public Accountant (CPA) is licensed by the state and has passed the CPA exam. A CPA can help you with tax preparation, financial statements, and advice on tax-related matters. Enrolled Agent (EA): EAs are tax professionals certified by the federal government. They specialize in tax preparation, tax planning, and representation before the IRS. They're a good choice if you're primarily concerned about tax issues.

2. **REFERRALS:** Ask fellow entrepreneurs, friends, or professionals like your lawyer or banker for referrals. Word of mouth can often lead to trusted professionals.

3. **INTERVIEW PROSPECTIVE ADVISORS:** Ask the right questions – ask about their experience, their fees and fee structure, their team's expertise, their approach to tax planning, and any specialties they might have. Some professionals might be aggressive in their tax strategies, while others might be more conservative. It's essential to find someone whose approach aligns with your comfort level.

4. **CONSIDER TECHNOLOGY AND COMMUNICATION:** In today's digital age, the best tax professionals use advanced software and online platforms to communicate and collaborate with clients. Ensure they use secure methods to exchange sensitive information and can provide services that fit your tech-savvy needs.

5. **FEES:** Understand their fee structure. Some charge by the hour, some have a fixed fee for services, and others might charge a percentage of your assets for ongoing financial planning.

6. **REGULAR CHECK-INS:** Once you hire someone, ensure that you have regular check-ins. The tax landscape and your business's financial situation can change, so ongoing communication is crucial.

Remember, the goal is to find someone who not only has the necessary expertise but also understands your business and personal financial goals. It's an important partnership, so take the time to choose the right person or firm to trust with your finances.

Mistake Six: This Book Can't Help Me

I understand that reading another business book may not be your top priority right now, but here's why this particular one might stand out:

1. **STRATEGIC WEALTH BUILDING:** Gain valuable insights into effectively managing and growing your personal wealth, enabling you to make informed decisions that positively impact your financial future.

2. **SIMPLIFIED CONCEPTS:** The book is crafted in a manner that simplifies complex tax concepts, making it accessible and easy to understand, regardless of your background or expertise in finance.

3. **FOCUS ON LONG-TERM PLANNING:** The book emphasizes the importance of long-term tax planning and financial management over quick-fix solutions, empowering you to develop a sustainable and resilient financial strategy for lasting success.

4. **PRACTICAL EXAMPLES:** Real-world case studies and practical examples shared in the book provide valuable context and application, allowing you to relate to the scenarios and apply the learnings to your specific business circumstances.

5. **TOP TIER** track record working with some of the world's most successful entrepreneurs- my experience and expertise in the tax and finance industry brings a unique perspective and depth of knowledge to the book, ensuring you receive insights and advice from a trusted and seasoned professional.

6. **EMPOWERMENT:** The overarching goal of the book is to equip you with the knowledge and tools needed to navigate the

complexities of the tax landscape confidently, enabling you to make well-informed financial decisions and drive your business toward greater success and sustainability.

I hope this book can be a valuable asset on your entrepreneurial journey.